Going
Postal

Going Postal

SCOTT MILZER

VILLARD
New York

Library of Congress Cataloging-in-Publication Data

Milzer, Scott.
    Going Postal: the 50 warning signs/Scott Milzer.—1st ed.
        p. cm.
    ISBN 0-679-77520-X
    1. Employee attitudes—Caricatures and cartoons.
  2. American wit and humor, Pictorial. I Title.
  NC1429.M57A4 1996
  741.5′ 973—dc20 96-9460

Random House website address:
http://www.randomhouse.com

Printed in the United States of America on acid-free paper

98765432

First Edition

Has the woman down the hall started wearing knitted sets of Kevlar shoulder pads?

Does the guy in the next cubicle cc all his correspondence to the Angel of Death?

Do your colleagues sacrifice live chickens at high-level meetings?

If you answered "yes" to any of these questions, then someone in your office may be on the verge of "going postal."

The warning signs of this affliction are unique. To date, fifty symptoms have been documented. There is no cure for this disease at present. The best advice: Lay low and hope for the best.

You can't be trusted with sharp objects.

WARNING SIGN

1

Your negotiation skills leave something
to be desired.

WARNING SIGN

2

Excessive use of Kevlar
shoulder pads.

WARNING SIGN

You begin micromanaging your employees.

WARNING SIGN

4

Excessive use of Post-its.

WARNING SIGN

5

A double latte just doesn't do it anymore.

WARNING SIGN

6

You're up to 62 packs a day —
and counting.

WARNING SIGN

7

You've been playing with dolls.

Clock-watching takes on a new dimension.

You have a look that kills.

You have trouble accepting your
performance evaluations.

WARNING SIGN

11

You start to work up a "Twinkie" defense.

WARNING SIGN

12

Small Talk of the Nearly Postal

WARNING SIGN

13

You take downsizing too literally.

You begin to dress inappropriately for work.

WARNING SIGN

15

You no longer "believe" in the need for anesthesia in dentistry.

WARNING SIGN

16

Too many hours staring in the window.

WARNING SIGN

17

You begin to answer to a higher authority.

WARNING SIGN

18

You change your eating habits.

WARNING SIGN

19

You find you're no longer a team player.

WARNING SIGN

20

You reach new depths of paranoia.

WARNING SIGN

21

There's a SWAT team to see you.

WARNING SIGN

22

Bunny slippers.

WARNING SIGN

23

THE LAST STRAW

THE POSTAL COMB-OVER

Hairstyles of the Nearly Postal

THE IMPLOSION

THE BUZZ WORD

WARNING SIGN

You get a tattoo.

Copying all letters to the angel of death.

Your memos become
inappropriately personal.

WARNING SIGN

You're spending too much time
in the water cooler.

WARNING SIGN

28

Your hands-on management style
is out of control.

Your boss is keeping you
on a shorter leash.

WARNING SIGN

30

Too many assertiveness training seminars.

WARNING SIGN

31

Misuse of office supplies.

Inanimate objects begin to reflect
your true feelings.

WARNING SIGN

33

Your job performance is but a shadow
of its former self.

Weapons of the Nearly Postal

WARNING SIGN

"Mr. Fisty" takes on more and more
of your work.

WARNING SIGN

36

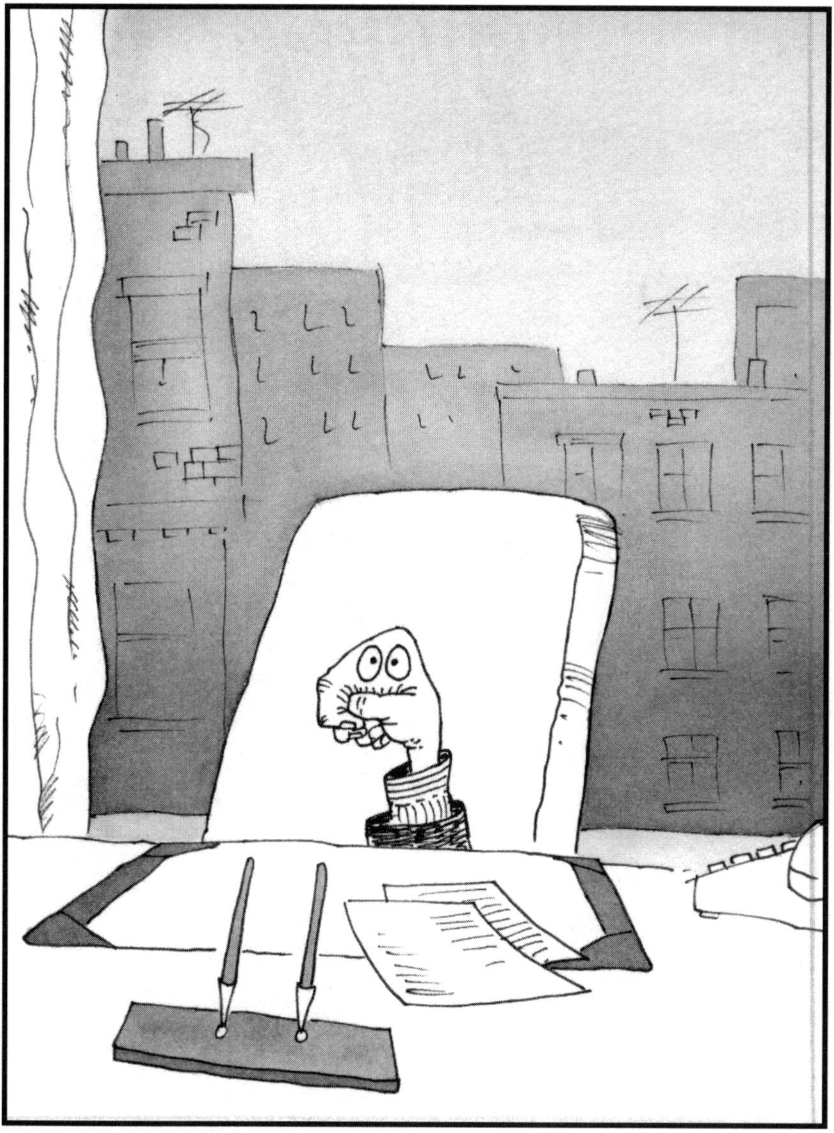

"Packing" for a business trip
takes on a whole new meaning.

WARNING SIGN

37

You're taking your work home with you.

You're no longer emotionally vested in your work.

WARNING SIGN

39

Indoor burning of office furniture.

WARNING SIGN

40

Suddenly your shoes are too tight.

WARNING SIGN

41

You perceive your co-workers as
"bio-hazards."

WARNING SIGN

42

Odd mistakes occur on the assembly line.

WARNING SIGN

43

You unintentionally verbalize all of your innermost thoughts.

WARNING SIGN

44

You paint your office black.

You harbor an irrational belief that others are talking about you.

WARNING SIGN

46

You harbor a rational belief that
others are talking about you.

WARNING SIGN

47

You rewire the elevator
during your lunch break.

WARNING SIGN

48

You begin drinking with the
nearly postal.

WARNING SIGN

Explosives of any sort taped to the body.

About the Illustrator

SCOTT MILZER is a quiet, unassuming fellow with a wry sense of humor. He is something of a loner. He keeps to himself, and has never *really* bothered anyone. When he's not cartooning, Scott likes to grind his teeth and listen to the thought commands of Azuzu, the Winged Goat-God of Nergal. We're not sure where he's from, although, as Scott wryly points out, that's none of our goddamned business.